FURY

David Morley is an ecologist and naturalist by background. He studied Zoology at the University of Bristol and pursued research on acid rain. His awards for poetry include the Ted Hughes Award and a Cholmondeley Award. He was elected a Fellow of the Royal Society of Literature in 2018. David is a Professor of Creative Writing at Warwick University. His work in education has been awarded a National Teaching Fellowship.

DAVID MORLEY

FURY

CARCANET

First published in Great Britain in 2020 by
Carcanet
Alliance House, 30 Cross Street
Manchester M2 7AQ
www.carcanet.co.uk

A CIP catalogue record for this book is
available from the British Library.

ISBN 978 1 78410 990 5

Book design by Andrew Latimer
Printed in Great Britain by SRP Ltd, Exeter, Devon

The publisher acknowledges financial
assistance from Arts Council England.

CONTENTS

First Lyrebird   3
The Thrown Voice   4
Romany Wounds Me   8
FURY   10
Second Lyrebird   13
What Will you Give for the Moon?   14
The Key Harvest   15
After the Burial of the Gypsy Matriarch   20
The Stuttering Butcher and the Sugarbeet King   21
Third Lyrebird   23
Wingbeats of a Romany Noun   24
Starling Roost in Swansea   25
'Like Wind through Woods in Riot'   27
'She is Leaf-like and Bird-like'   29
Orphans of Orphans   32
Fourth Lyrebird   33
Honour   34
When I Heard the Calling of Birds   36
Cockade   38
Rafter   39
Fifth Lyrebird   40
Gamekeeper's Ghost   41
Significance at Innominate Tarn   42
The Apostle Birds   43
I Dropt Down on the Thymy Molehill   45
Sixth Lyrebird   46
The Caravans of Tarshish   47
    1st caravan   48
    2nd caravan   50
    3rd caravan   52
    4th caravan   55

5th caravan   58
6th caravan   62
7th caravan   65
scattered to the rims of wide england   69
Kop Kop to His Horses He Sings and No More   72
Cherry Pickers   73
Our Home is a Hunger   75
Gypsies   76
Seventh Lyrebird   77
Translations from a Stammerer   78
   after a phrase by Anna Akhmatova   78
   after a phrase by Osip Mandelshtam   78
   after a phrase by Paul Celan   79
   after a phrase by Bronisława Wajs   79
   after a phase by Marina Tsvetaeva   79
   after a phrase by Vladimir Mayakovsky   80
   after a phrase by Bronisława Wajs   80
   after a phrase by John Keats   81

Notes   83
Acknowledgements   90

FURY

FIRST LYREBIRD

Your vow is the Lyrebird's thesaurus of mimicry.
Your vow yaffles with the laughter of a Kookaburra.

Your vow sings the syllables you share with our children.
Your vow lullabies a jungle's stories, canopies, and understory.

My vow catapults a Kingfisher past a Kookaburra.
My vow scales a frozen waterfall's icicled aviary.

My vow strips a eucalypt's paperbark for nests for Rainbow Lorys.
My vow ploughs a ridge-walk through a peat-bog's slog and slurry.

Your vow paints Jane Austen's miniatures on two inches of ivory.
Your vow quickens a bare forest with your footsteps in snow.

Your vow spills its watershed through the fell's tarns and freshets
and startles snowdrops from the floor of heaven.

My vow hushes a fir forest and my footsteps in snow.
My vow spies a single star from out the wide night's numbers.

THE THROWN VOICE
Romany

'The story starts with who you are.
I strode at night across the heath to hear
a nightjar. It was night which throws
her voice inside a bird. I would stand below
his song and become cast into creature,
into his purled world. The bird could never
be seen. It seemed a soft scar of sound
as if a lone tree's bark sang the night's wound
from a lone tree's bough, and yet heath
and bird were grown two in the dark.
Those wound, wounded voices were thrown
into me, as if bird and tree were hornbooks
I could finger and trace and sing aloud.
I spoke through night, or night through me
and all the creatures of the night sang free.
My Gypsies gave tongue to campfire stories
but my spell drew speech from the circling heath.
I was a magician to them, the magic man
to my people. I lost it. I lost my magic
when I lost those voices. I cried my eyes out.
I have cried my eyes into myself. How can
you know what it is like to lose your magic?'

The magician drains his hipflask of whiskey.
I catch him under his thin arms and catch myself
in surprise, for he weighs no more than a bird,
as though the bones were air-blown, his body
a wingspan, not a man. I cradle him to earth.
'What's gone can be gained again', he whispers,
'Take the path across the purling heath;

night-long, overhear the notes of nightfall,
nocturne of nightjars turning with the world
from county to county in slown song:
a slur of notes played without departure
or border. There's the thrown voice you seek:
to be thrown into pure bird, poured song, hear
the soft scar of the night's wound. Let me rest'.

A young Gypsy winks at me: 'Take no notice
of the sly old soak. It's the DTs blathering
through him now. He can't get his act together
by which we mean his *Act*. That shaman blether
is stabbing him in the liver. This broken bottle.
That smashed bottle there. The spirit's spirited away
his spirit'. The Gypsies laugh. 'He made mad magic
before the booze,' another smiles. 'The man
could pirouette playing cards on his palm,
flip the whole pack up to burst like doves,
flapped down as one bird into the dovecote
of his fist. One bird! At our winter fairs
he'd dance the crowd on the marionette strings
of his voice. No prop or pose. Not even a song.
Now he's the maddened ghost of his act…'.
'Uncle!' a teenage Gypsy jeers, 'are you sleeping
or waking? – or still fast in the fumes
of the whiskey-world between dream and dram?
Look at those dregs in his cup. He can't read
a word or world from them not for love nor money.
Maybe he might, brothers – for another swig!'
The Gypsy spits: 'He capers in the majesty

of magic when he's smashed. He's pissed away
his craft but it's us who've counted the cost.'
The magician weeps and gropes into wet grass.

An elder Gypsy rises from his heels:
'You will not join in laughing at the man.
It is gentle of you: to read past
his sadness and madness. We forge
our memory of what he was, not
what he has become. He was the first
magician and fortune-forger of our tribe.
The leaf-teller and palm-reader of his time.
The man could take your hand into his fist,
and read you like a book. He would wrestle
your heart and rummage through your soul.
The elder holds out his work-worn palms.
"Our hands are the books of what we have lived" –
This is what the magician preached on Sundays
– the one day he was dry. It was holy
to him in saying, and to us. "One palm",
he would cry, "is scripture we have yet to write."
Life lines and Fate lines. Love lines. Marriage lines.
Yet the man, like us, could read no book-words.
He reads himself in the speech of his tears.
Get this tortured creature to his bed.'

They haul him tottering and lurching
to his feet and, half-joking, coaxing,
carry him legless to his caravan.
The magician stares through me:
'I cannot hear the nightjar: my heart's bird,
the thrown voice, his song of no words.
All my animals moved on from me
as if I were an ark axed to splinters

on my Ararat. I lost them. Smashed
my magic. Go back there: pace the path
down my mountain of error below
the snowline, the triggered tracks of white hares.
At nightfall, lay yourself on the heather
beneath the lone fir; listen for his purling,
turning a world without words'. His eyes
slide into themselves, a snail's horns.
The Gypsies wrestle him to the ground
as a seizure wracks him. 'Our hands
are open books of what we have lived,'
he raves. 'Do you want to read me?
Do you want to read my life?'

He holds out his hands.
He holds out his trembling hands.

ROMANY WOUNDS ME

after George Seferis's 'In the Manner of G.S.'
for Damian Le Bas

Wherever I travel, Romany wounds me.
As I hoved into the horse fair at Stow-on-the-Wold
between Cotswold chintz shops and the roving road
HGVs hunkered after our wagons on the Fosse Way
cursing us with airbrakes and grunting gearshifts.
At Kenilworth fair, with its tailbacks to Longbridge roundabout,
vardos bottle-necked behind ponies from Pershore,
rocks rammed on verges of all the villages between
by Neighbourhood Watches with the policeman's nod.
At Dereham fair I crow-barred the stern stones from the wayside
and flattened fat molehills under my 4 x 4
and snored under the stars of headlights flying across the bypass
and slung the crook of my kettle above an illegal blaze.
At Gressenhall, Swaffham, and Peterborough
the pubs were barred to me.
What do the Gentiles want, these polite people
who curse us we're Romanian or worse than?
A copper pulls us over and barks for passports.
'Mate, I come from Rotherham', laughs one Gypsy,
'though it's foreign country round these parts'.
And as we sleep Europe drifts away across the sea.
The cling-net of England closes. Our caravans are ships
with their engines flooded. Our lives are drowning.
Strange people, the English. They say, 'this land is ours'
but they don't rove beyond their commutes or school runs.
Imagine the coppers rocking up at their caravan sites!
Meanwhile, England keeps on travelling, always travelling backwards.
In my dream, our flotilla of caravans sets sail from Dover's chalk shore
as though the little boats of Dunkirk were our own Gypsy vardos,

as though we were machine-gunned by our own spitfires,
and those brothers on the beach were our own strafed kin,
which we were, when we were borderless and one.
Between the horse fairs of Horsmonden and Appleby
at all the stopping places when I wake, and in every face I see,
wherever I travel, Romany wounds me.

Stow-on-the-Wold, Kenilworth, Dereham, Horsmonden and Appleby are
traditional Traveller horse fairs.

FURY

'I love talking.'

– Tyson Fury, British Romany professional boxer

The fight's over. My corner-man and cut-man
are mist and water, mist and slaughter.
I scream at the crowd and swagger to the exit.
I bow my face in a locker-room mirror,
and to the mirror behind my eyes.
Infinity. A million beaten faces
stare out, blazing back at me,
brains black-puddinged from pummelling.
My fists are beating the locker door.
I am fighting-royalty. I have Gypsy
kings on both sides of the family.
My three brothers are the same as me.
With us, everyone is a tough guy.
They don't talk like you and me
are talking. But we all cry instantly.
Look at me: 6 feet 9. If someone
said this to me in my family,
I would just cry. All of us would.
But nothing's talked about in our family.
We just push each other aside,
or give each other a punch.
We don't bow to any man.
The red mist rises, an invisible
cloak around my ringside robe.
We won't bow to you.
I bow to the red mist, naked as fury.
It's not about the money fights.
It's the love of one-on-one combat,
the ring entrances, the talking.

I'm the Master of It all.
When I go in there, I'm trying
to put my fist through the back
of his head. To break his ribs,
make them sob out the other side.
Final bell. I bow to the mist, being gone.
I feel a chill burning my skin.
When the red mist rises, I see
their faces, as many as my mind's eye
can remember. I'd give my right arm
for any man who stays on his toes.
I'm in control when out of control.
The best style is no style.
You take a little something from everything,
use what works, chuck the rest out the ring.
My game's to get your man on the ground –
sprawl-and-brawl, grind-and-pound.
Gum-shield and teeth, they're one to me.
Once down, don't get up from your knees.
This is not your celeb boxing.
It's felling the other chancer in the ring
short of butchering the bastard
before he gets his breath back,
before he begs for no more.
One clean blow and the mist
will part for him. My opponent begs
for mercy. What's that, pal?
I'm Fury. Who's this Mercy?
The breath goes up from the beaten
ghost of a man. Submission.
I'll tell you who Fury is.
Eye to eyeball at the mirror;

breath on the screen while I scream
at replays on my iPad.
Pal,
one minute I'm inside the sun
and the next I'm in my car, gunning it
into a wall at a hundred miles an hour.
I don't trust you as far as I could
throw you. I don't trust myself.
I bought a brand-new Ferrari
in the summer of 2016.
I was bombing up the motorway
got the beast up to 190mph
heading smack towards a bridge.
I heard a voice crying,
your kids, your family,
your sons and daughter
growing up without their dad.
Before I turned into the bridge
I skidded back on the hard shoulder.
I have been so dark everything was pitch-black.
The fight's over. My corner-man and cut-man
are mist and water, mist and slaughter.
There is a name for what I am. I scream it
at the crowd and stagger to the exit.

ξ

SECOND LYREBIRD

My vow scissors wildflowers and presses their heavens.
My vow calculates backward, slides sideways to the finite.

Your vow zooms a telescope's zoetrope of meteor showers.
Your vow rides comet-tails through the dark matter.

Your vow severs calculus and abacus; your now is infinite.
Your vow eavesdrops Wisława Szymborska typing, 'I don't know.'

My vow is wordlessness, its silence an echo chamber.
My vow unravels a paraglider through one thousand metres.

My vow muses with Elizabeth Bishop's grandmother, '… nobody knows.'
My vow computes chaos theory in a cacophony of cockatoos.

Your vow ravels up a Raven's thermals to ten thousand metres
and vaults between the fling and grasp of a trapeze.

Your vow is a Wedge-tailed Eagle, wild above an open-air zoo.
Your vow is a Noh Play of Samurai Caddisflies.

The Traveller seeks the key-harvester:
artist of mort and mortice,
miller, planer, sharpener of sorrows,

with a thousand keys to ways not taken.
The key harvester holds a cold coin in her hand.
She lifts her gaze from her sparking lathe.

Why is a moon misting in her palm?
The lathe's steel scream stutters to silence.
Her keys, tempered, cool like comets

on hooks of orbit, twinkling, astigmatic.
The coin, the moon, is her new pressing.
What do you pay for with a moon?

What will you give for a moon? she asks the Traveller.
Her cat, as if to prove cats know, arches his spine
and twines his tail around her ankles, leonine,

languidly lingering under her fingers…
Moonlight plays with reflections in a mirror.
The cat pounces on a moonbeam on the floor.

The light, startled, skitters below a table.
The cat noses and paws at her vanished prey
but the moon stares from the dark. The lathe gleams.

What will you give for the moon? asks the mirror.

THE KEY HARVEST
Romany

I stoop, stepping over a stile, through
head-high mayflower in a hawthorn hedgerow

to a Travellers' site writhed in campfire smoke,
steam streaming from spouts of kettles on crooks,

hens skittering with their fluff-chicks under caravans.
The key harvester's door is drawn wide;

the woman slight as a steadied chisel, lips pursed in a vice.
The Travellers frown up from their fry-ups and fires.

The key-harvester grimaces towards them:
'Gypsies passing through. Ignore them. Speak.

What you need from me.' Behind her the keys
winking from hooks in the bow-top, a spick and span

single bed. This is all. All she needs.
'Come up, man.' She shifts lightly to the bunk

with eyes aslant among a silver harvest of keys.
'For all your rapping at my door', she declares,

'a door is a wall of stone. I stare a lock through it,
unbolt it with my eye. This mortise is no eye

for your key but for my own. In unlatched dark
I unlock my art's agility.' She sits astride

her cutting wheel, one fist clenched white;
fingers of her other hand bladed and straight.

'I can see the key needed for you, mind.
I can craft its cam and magic chamfers.'

She rummages through a toolbox
and draws out a deadlock.

'This is what's become of your heart.
A spring-lock slithers side to side

– so does my sight and my oiled hands –
when you crank the key to clockwise.

By the gift of my pins and tumblers
you swivel the cam, shoot the steel

and pull the door into the dark.
Now, throw the bolt. Draw out my art.'

She spreads her palms upward like an actor.
The key harvester strides sideways through the door

as though slipping offstage to the wings:
'There is a gift for you. She too's been tarrying.'

The woman leaps around the back of her van,
sidles back leading a foal Gypsy cob.

She sweeps one hand along the Piebald's hind.
'Fetlock to wedlock, darling of my heart,

she is mane, mine, soul's reason I placed warm cash
on her and wool-gathered in her foaling place.

I would have been gone – three months since –
but she loves the sweet grazing grass by the burn,

her singing water. Love tethers me to her stake.
See –', the woman swivels to where I stand,

'my palms are tempered through lack of labour,
my purse is dry from a drought of trading.'

She passes the lead-rope to me. 'She is yours now'.
'I have no knack for horses', I cry, 'Why gift her to me?'

'Look at my people', she nods towards the Gypsies,
'pretending to be free. Hark at yourself,

forging freedom in their poverty.
They are locked in lives by lies of their forefathers.

Their Gypsy elders are their fetters not their betters.
I did not want this life. I fought my father bare-knuckle.

My mother was no mother but a fairground magpie:
thief to truth, leading all her brood up the roads.

To tell life as lie, tooth, nail: lock it in your kids.
I forged my way from father and mother,

brother and sister. As soon as I was ten
I held my ground in this driven world.

I am what their savage loving has made me.
Gypsies, fires, stopping places – dirt, dread and dysentery.

I was having none of them, except none would have me
in the unturning world – because *I* was Gypsy,

so *I* was dirt. I made my road, half out, half nowt,
nothing whole so, to prise the black hole's door

of myself, I rasped a key: a talent for turning
tiny gears of iron into the tinny souls you're hearing

jangling from gibbets in my caravan.
I wanted nothing. To be – nothing. I wanted

nothing to be nothing, to live by no thing.
To smelt the solder between the weld of things:

of men, women, children. Every door in me
was slammed to them – although I knew the key.

Each time I cut myself off, I hung the key
in the chill wake of my van; but for every key

I chiselled a copy and made it a gift
to any soul who could not see their way

to love or joy or life. I knew my loneliness
was stronger than the pulse of love.

I harvested silence for myself, and the space
for one soul – held fast by ten thousand keys.

As my caravan rumbles and rattles along
rutted lanes and cobbles, the keys clatter

in glad rejection, reminding me
I have no door to fling wide or fasten,

no daughter or son, no home but what I carry.'
The woman weighs the deadlock in her palm:

'It is a heavy heart, your heart!' She smiles thinly.
'This pony,' the Gypsy sighs, 'she has smashed

my magic locks. My ajar soul stamps and romps
through all my opened doors. She makes me dream

of what I might have been: a part of a world,
not apart from it.' She whispers, sharply:

'I cannot have her near me when I am at my worst.
I have no gift for love: I can skill it out for you

if you take this pony.' Lightly, she strokes
the ear tufts of the cob. 'Even when you try',

she turns to me, 'you're no Gypsy. I trust nobody
– but trust you not to hurt or barter her.

She is your key.' I take the pony by her tether
and bind in two her twine around my wrist.

The Gypsy gazes past me into the paths of stars:
'She is Venus who stares down to us staring back at her.'

She stoops through a closing door and slams the bolt.

AFTER THE BURIAL OF THE GYPSY MATRIARCH
marime vôrdòn

The Roma are torching her proud vardo in mirnomos.
The yag leaps into the bóro and billows in mirnomos.
Páto, tsáliya, pátura: her possessions flare in mirnomos.
Her raklo shuffles her bánka, palms them out in mirnomos.
The yag leaps into the bóro and billows in mirnomos.

Her lurcher is nashaval from the kámpo in mirnomos.
Her raklo shuffles her bánka, palms them out in mirnomos.
The zhukûl peers and peers from the wûsh in mirnomos.
Her lurcher is nashaval from the kámpo in mirnomos.
Pàrrâ tower to their kríza, collapse in mirnomos.

The zhukûl peers and peers from the wûsh in mirnomos.
The Roma rake and rake the skrúma in mirnomos.
Pàrrâ tower to their kríza, collapse in mirnomos.
Their vardos circle the field. They vanish in mirnomos.
The Roma rake and rake the skrúma in mirnomos.

What the Roma do not say to each other is buried in mirnomos.
Their vardos circle the field. They vanish in mirnomos.
Páto, tsáliya, pátura: everything burns in mirnomos.
What the Roma do not say to each other is buried in mirnomos.
The Roma are torching her vardo. Everything must burn.

After death, the home and belongings of a Roma Gypsy are considered mahrime, 'unclean', and are burnt. **Romani:** English: **marime vôrdòn:** contaminated wagon; **vardo:** Gypsy caravan; **mirnomos:** silence; **yag:** fire; **bóro:** oak; **páto:** bed; **tsáliya:** clothing; **pátura:** bedclothes; **raklo:** son; **bánka:** banknotes; **nashaval:** chased away; **kámpo:** camp; **zhukûl:** hound; **wûsh:** woodland; **pàrrâ:** flames; **kríza:** crisis; **skrúma:** ashes.

20

THE STUTTERING BUTCHER AND THE
SUGARBEET KING

It used to be a thing of porridge in the morning
and you never had nothing to work on.
  – Wisdom Smith, Gypsy

I knows what night is to leave my wife in bed
     when the moon swings up, silvering, and go
ferreting all moon-time to fetch up conies,
     hawk them sixpence a piece, bag the skin back.
We trussed them to the stuttering butcher
     at Oaksey out by Crudwell.
We let him have conies half-a-crown a piece.
     The skin making eighteen pence.
When Gorgio mushe's merripen and Romany Chal's
     merripen wels kettaney, kek kosto merripen see.

When we'd finished the hops we gads down
     around Ross-on-Wye to The Sugarbeet King.
He'd romp round and rein the jobs,
     sugarbeet pulling and mangle shawing.
Toiling and shawing. Tailing and topping.
     That's back work! Me and the gang of us.
We had to tump them up, the sugarbeet,
     shaw them buggers all up the row.
When Gorgio mushe's merripen and Romany Chal's
     merripen wels kettaney, kek kosto merripen see.

When you finished, you had to spin
        around and fettle them all into heaps
to come and pick them up with tractor
        and trailer. Nowadays, they gaff around
with harvester, and haulm-roller tumps them,
        pulls them, beats them, tops them, the lot.
Tails them and topples them in the separator.
        I'll tell you the truth, it spoils the sport!
When Gorgio mushe's merripen and Romany Chal's
        merripen wels kettaney, kek kosto merripen see.

A spoken Gypsy Ballad adapted from an interview with the Gypsy folk-singer Wisdom ['Wiggy'] Smith, Gypsy, 1926–2001, by Gwilym Davies, *Folk Music Journal*, Annual 2004. 'When Gorgio mushe's merripen and Romany Chal's merripen wels kettaney, kek kosto merripen see': 'When the Gentile way of living and the Gypsy way of living come together, it is anything but a good way of living'.

ξ

THIRD LYREBIRD

My vow steadies the circus ladder skying above an acrobat's apprentice.
  My vow precipitates Arcus, Wall Cloud and Pyrocumulus.

My vow yawns the dawn chorus's enormous Yes.
  My vow will never master the art of loss.

Your vow condenses Stratus, Cirrus, and Altocumulus.
  Your vow sees worlds in grains of sand, heavens in wildflowers.

Your vow is Elizabeth Bishop inviting Marianne Moore 'please come flying'.
  Your vow spills a chimera over an octopus's electric coat.

My vow is a desert bloom in Sahara, Rub' al Khali, and Atacama.
  My vow serves the Great White Shark's vendetta against inertia.

My vow courts cuttlefish under sprawled robes of ink
  and holes-up in a hermit crab's hollowed-out hermitage.

Your vow swerves with a Blue Shark's pressure-waves of prey.
  Your vow lights the red shift of the Andromeda Galaxy.

WINGBEATS OF A ROMANY NOUN

flightpath of a micro-moth   *phakalo móyohorro*

wingbeats of its noun   *o phakh hurimos anav*

snared by lamp-light   *si chórdyol andral yog*

of my tongue by your tongue   *pa ki Inglezítska*

STARLING ROOST IN SWANSEA
Angloromani

Andesára of starlings. All of them sleepy head
   chiriklòs barikanò, buff-glossy
      on zhútso and rukh bicker to wavver

in their tenement wesh of Swansea têmnomós...
   Martiya. Rom John slows his vardo in the slush
      into the hush-a-by NCP, kills the lampash.

Drom khatinênde.
   Rom John pockets his gîndo:
      zhanimos of this atching-tan for the ryat

with no brother-vardo or mukker in sight,
   no zhuko yakh for the gadji or zgandáriya.
      A Roma's luck's lovênge in his djépo.

Rom John rifles a manrrorro of moolah
   – ziiiiiiip! – as he pad-pads ratyáko
      about his blunt bíznizo:

wúzho pai, siphoned – husssh! – from the garage's kránto,
   cigs scored from the raklorro behind the night-grille,
      and a starlichimásko slash under the starry wûsh!

Pissheads waddling home – igam ogam! – fisticuffing fanári
street steep to their feet, eavesdropping vuzheyimos
of a bateríya heating the Rom's kalisfériya...

One khulalo gadjo thumps a filástra, fist-pumps the vardo,
forcing a *come-on* from our sleep-dead, snoring Rom.
Ach, John, man! Hear him – xûrimós – xûrimós – xûrimós –

under a riot of starlings, a ryat of Swansea starlings!

Romani: English: **andesára**: twilight; **chiriklòs**: birds; **barikanò**: puffed-up;
zhútso: wire; **rukh**: tree; **wavver**: to one another; **wesh**: forest; **têmnomós**:
darkness; **Martiya**: spirits of the night; **Rom**: Gypsy man; **vardo**: van; **lampash**:
headlights; **drom khatinênde**: a road to nowhere; **gîndo**: suspicions; **zhanimos**:
wisdom; **atching-tan**: stopping-place; **ryat**: night; **zhuko yakh**: pair of eyes;
gadji: non-Roma people; **zgandáriya**: the police; **lovênge**: cash; **djépo**: pocket;
manrrorro: roll; **ratyáko**: nightly: **bíznizo**: business; **wúzho pai**: drinking water;
kránto: outside tap; **raklorro**: young bloke; **starlichimásko**: radiant; **wûsh**: tree;
fanári: streetlamps; **vuzheyimos**: humming (n); **bateríya**: car battery; **kalisfériya**:
netherworld; **khulalo**: shitty; **gadjo**: non-Romany man; **filástra**: window;
xûrimós: snores; **ryat**: night.

'LIKE WIND THROUGH WOODS IN RIOT'
'On Wenlock Edge' in Angloromani

Wenlock Edge, o well-narked wêrsh;
   o Wrekin whoosed o wûsh bakrêski-morki;
oh, turbo-charged turbáto balwal, o kangarooing kashtorro,
   ai del o viv patrins pe o Severn.

Phúrdel e balwal bonkers ándo National Trust wêrshorró
   desar Róma anzardo catatonic Uriconium:
o phurano balwal andre o raven-raw roadkill
   núma balwal molotil avér wêrsh.

Éta, Roma! Do-multano, o schizoid soldáta
   o yakh plivîl-pe o warzone of Shropshire.
Same old, same old: yekh-fyálo Indiana Jones,
   yekh-fyálo sokotimos milwares si...

Phúrdel e balwal, o phurdayimos shoro,
   balwal pa naff National Trust gift-shop;
chi mai shtum o kasht-manushikanimos
   yekh-fyálo buki si, bullshit buki si...

Oh, turbo-charged turbáto balwal, o comatose kashtorro.
   O phurano balwal kovlyol.
Éta, landlocked Róma! Skrúma telal English Heritage.
   Éta, landless Roma! Our harked Hiraeth...

Angloromani: English: **wêrsh**: wood; **wûsh**: forest; **bakrêski-morki**:
fleece(n); **turbáto balwal**: gale; **kashtorro**: saplings; **ai del o viv**: it is
blizzarding; **patrins**: leaves (n); **pe**: on; **phúrdel e balwal**: it is blowing;
ándo: into; **wêrshorró**: copse; **desar**: since; **Róma**: Rome; **anzardo**: built;

andre: within; **núma**: but; **molotil**: thresh; **aver**: different; **Éta**: Look!; **Roma**: Romani tribe; **do-multano**: long ago; **soldáta**: soldier; **yakh**: eye; **plivîl-pe**: afloat on; **yekh-fyálo buki si**: it is the same thing ('plus ça change', 'same old, same old'); **sokotimous**: thought; **milwares**: thousandfold; **phurdayimos**: windstorm/riot of wind; **shoro**: life; **pa**: through; **chi mai**: never; **kasht-manushikanimos**: tree of mankind; **kovlyol**: abate; **skrúma**: ashes; **telal**: below; **Hiraeth**: longing for homeland (Welsh/Welsh Romani).

'SHE IS LEAF-LIKE AND BIRD-LIKE'

Sani hai chiriklani si – Romany

I.

Támna trees are kited and tailed
by milwares patrins in pell-mell

that stretch their necks on stalks
shelo-snapping before spinning

lighting the fields with linnets strewn
and drawn in murmuration;

unwinding núvaros, flowing skutsome
to skat-scatters of bird-thought:

a skyfalling cavalry, a swooning avali:

          kaleni kasht!
  wérsh wifflcr!
             bóro!
  lólochirillo!
      kalo kanrro!
    fazáno!
              pendexin!
  romanichirrilo!

Romani: English: '**Sani hai chiriklani si**': 'she is leaf-like and bird-like'; **támna:** autumn; **milwares:** a thousandfold; **patrin:** leaf, also means a page; **shelo:** rope; **núvaro:** cloud; **skutsome:** alert; **avali:** yes; **kaleni kasht:** blackberry bush; **wérsh wiffler:** woodpigeon; **bóro:** oak; **lólochirillo:** redpoll; **kalo kanrro (mamuxar):** blackthorn; **fazáno:** pheasant; **pendexin:** hazel; **romanichirrilo:** water wagtail.

29

2.

Patrins flicker across char,
wagtailing amboldimásko

skydiving, hedge-delving
with head-banging yellowhammers

pounded by breshûndomós.

Flitting through helved light

in a hedge, those patrin-chiriklòs
wren-wrapped in patrin-porr

bowled around boles of hedgerows:

           yelmalin!
bittikánni!
             gyandelin!
sapêsko-chiriklos!
              búrcho!
     chiplitárka!
yêldelin!
          spátso!

amboldimásko: swirling; breshûndomós: rain-storm; patrin-chiriklòs: leaf-birds; patrin-porr: leaf-feather; yelmalin: elm; bittikánni: patridge; gyandelin: beech; sapêsko-chiriklo: yellow hammer; búrcho: birch tree; chiplitárka: woodpecker; yêldelin: elder tree; spátso: sparrow.

3.

The chiripimos kumpania
crash-diving in deciduous

cacophonous colour-fest,
brichíris-rainbows of chlorophyll;

their wind-wrung Rrayo:
their detonated aviary.

A turbo turbáto
hauls a tree's fury weather-wards

from kakya lúmiya, into the nether worlds:

    plopelin!
               chiriklí-mulikani!
     sêlka!
          kalo chiriklo!
  sikamúra!
           chuhuriyézo!
  kasht-kovlo!
             kakaráchi!

chiripimos: twittering; kumpania: tribe; brichíris: rainbows; Rrayo: Afterworld; turbáto: gale; kakya lúmiya: the next world; plopelin: poplar; chiriklí-mulikani: nightjar; sêlka: willow; kalo chiriklo: blackbird; sikamúra: sycamore; chuhuriyézo: tawny owl; kasht-kovlo: ash tree; kakaráchi: magpie.

ORPHANS OF ORPHANS

As I turn the tilth of my garden
two courting robins gang up beside me.

A nature poem. Yet I must seem to them
a symbiont wrecker of temples.

I shift planters, displace a populace.
From under their squat temples

woodlice-worlds spill from hovels.
All animals are orphans: the robins

rip through the woodlice in frenzy.
Centipedes back-peddle their oars;

the birds catch by their gold antennae.
They tear them to pieces, swallow them alive.

Sunlight slides over country by country,
slab by slab. A nature poem.

ξ

Your vow conducts the Anemone's three-ring circus of Clownfish.
 Your vow gives the colours' desire to Frida Kahlo.

My vow kites in the red drift of migrating Monarch Butterflies.
 My vow divines the jangled language of migrating geese.

My vow captures the colour Kahlo desired of Diego de Rivera.
 My vow meshes and rings winged verbs in mist-nets.

Your vow deciphers the driftwood's pictographs and hicroglyphs.
 Your vow braids a belt of straw, ivy buds, and coral clasps.

Your vow releases Orioles from their snares and lime-traps.
 Your vow frets a Nightingale's dulcimer at dawn.

My vow unclasps a coral reef from its bleached atoll
 and clenches an oak leaf in free-fall.

My vow is a Tawny Owl packing up his piccolo at dawn.
 My vow plies a Goldfinch's splattered palette and easel.

HONOUR
after Ovid

Opopanax, balsam,
      bdellium, guggul, bisabol –
scented resins of myrrh,
      the pitiful tears of Myrrha
who fled from Cinyras,
      from the bride-bed of her father.
Over nine moons of waning,
      she roused in a village in Arabia,
their child Adonis swelling,
      a stone in the apricot of her,
that sapling of her lust
      planted in her by her father.
By adulterous Cinyras.
      No god uproots his future.
Stained Myrrha, daughter, praying.
      One god conjures his answer.
Which is to bring the women elders
      of the village with their razors
to slam her down, splayed,
      to sever her of pleasure;
to abandon the girl, bleeding,
      in the grace of that god's favour
in the grave-grove of his Sahara
      in answer to her poor prayer.
That god's pity is a cess of leaves
      spilling over Myrrha's shoulders;
his pity is her toes tearing roots
      into the midden beneath her;
his pity is her slight limbs straitening
      into her fingerprints' growth rings;

his pity is needles of lignin
          eviscerating her viscera;
his pity is the auxin of shame
          stealing across her synapses,
the photosynthesis of breath
          making her every word vapour.
Silence at the heartwood of her heart.
          Silence of the leaves of her palms,
the drip-tips of her fingertips.
          Silence of her arteries furring with phloem,
of this sapwood of her skin,
          of her death-mask of lichen.
And as the slow bark's sprawl
          swallowed Myrrha, closing
over her hair, that god,
          her father, whispered:
Beloved Myrrha. Daughter.
I did this. For your honour.

WHEN I HEARD THE CALLING OF BIRDS
For Towfiq Bihani

When I heard the calling of birds, I remembered your sweet voice when you sang
the song 'remember me this way'.
– Towfiq Bihani, Guantánamo Bay detainee

I remembered your sweet voice when you sang, 'remember me this way'.
When you folded my heart in your wing to remember me this way.

When emerald hummingbirds flashed through the chain-link fence,
I remembered them that day.

When a palm swift slipped from her nest in the dark of Camp Echo,
I remembered and counted that day.

When lazuli buntings burst in a blue cloud above my open-sky cage,
I remembered and blessed their day.

When saffron finches dust-bathed in the detention yard,
I dreamed of home that day.

When I heard rapid-fire of woodpeckers in the pines below Camp Echo,
I remembered and trembled that day.

When I saw scarlet tanagers swoop across the gulf of Guantánamo,
I fled with them that day.

When the oriole bowed his orange cowl from the watchtower,
I remembered and feared that day.

When stygian owls plied their sorrow-flutes in reeds beyond the kill-zone,
I remembered and wept that day.

When a mourning dove swayed on her roost of razor-wire above Camp Echo,
I buried my heart that day.

I wake to macaws squawking *Towfiq*, the echo of guards bawling *Bohani*.
My heart is folded in your wing. Remember me this way.

COCKADE

Meero dado, soskey were creminor kair'd?
Meero chauvo, that puvo-baulor might job by halling lende.
Dad, why were worms made? Boy, so moles might live.
    – Romany saying

'Dad, why were worms made?' 'Boy, so moles
might live. And you and me live by trapping moles,
stabbing their berry noses on barbed wire
where they flap and drip through winter on winter.
Felt souls. Had I time or mind to consider
the blameless creatures we have bagged and spiked
I may come to thinking our living too costly
for half their slaughter. Let us not go circling
questions as though one thing feeds another.
Nothing I know in the woodland gnaws on questions.
Sling me my mallet and pegs and let us stake our traps so.'
So, my father bent his soul among leaf-mould,
tapped, turned and tightened his traps but reached out
one hand to me, sighing, 'Son, we shall not gain by knowing.
Let us spring wide the jaws of our gins, bide quietly
by our yog and wait out this night's frost together.'
When he had done, he lifted his hat, swept its cockade about him,
saluting one by one the snare-holes where my questions slept.

Yog: campfire

38

RAFTER

After he died my father palmed his body from the ash.
He lifted it to our loft where he shivered on a rafter
four yards above my pillow, daring me to ask
or reach through that kicked crack in the ceiling plaster.

ξ

FIFTH LYREBIRD

Your vow snags a maple-key on spinning wind-flow.
  Your vow rattles a berserker Wren, outbattling all rivals.

Your vow unpicks the fossicking Goldfinches from their teasel.
  Your vow pecks in the gravel with John Keats's house sparrows.

My vow kens a Wren's kenning, dweller of a caved-in well.
  My vow snares a Mantis praying for escape-artist spiders.

My vow flickers with Fanny Brawne's butterflies in shadows.
  My vow pings a tuning-fork in a zither of zinging mayflies.

Your vow warps the weft of a Dewdrop Spider's spinnerets.
  Your vow stirs a millpond's mirror and stills a heron's after-image.

Your vow smooths a Quetzal's emerald crown cresting her tail-banners
  and somersaults among the Starlings' murmuration.

My vow skulks with quag-creeping Crakes and Water Rails.
  My vow tricks the optic nerve between Quetzal and invisibility.

GAMEKEEPER'S GHOST

'Judge the wood judge the gamekeeper' – Romany saying

What do these wood ants want from me?
They shear my shirts of unwinding skin.

Nature's gentlemen at their sprack tasks;
mine-ropes of ants hauling me hollow.

A shot split the wood. I slunk to a cedar's
cover alert as a hart. Poacher held hard. Court

of oak and ash. My word and hand and hound
against his. I wrung every hare from him.

I got jumped in Woodcote Lane after the lock-in.
Seven mates or his kin, ach, I know them.

Snoring snowman, I slumbered under sleet.
Raw winds freezing my wrists and fists.

Self-snared in snowy woods I prayed
I had spared the hares of heaven.

SIGNIFICANCE AT INNOMINATE TARN

from my notebooks for 'The Impact of Acid Rain on Freshwater Insects
in Tarns of the English Lake District', unpublished PhD thesis

In Innominate Tarn the
significance of mortality can vary
anywhere between 90% and 95%. I
weighed the significance

of my lover's final word to me,
rearranging the letters in the hope
of a buried code, of meaning, of
movement, of radiance.

The diversity of bloodworms
narrows, given even slight changes
in the acidity of precipitation. The
shame in me

saw only the narrowness of my
lover's face, thinned by cigarettes to
a staring skeleton.

The collapse of fish numbers from
acid rain correlates with a collapse
of insect larval communities. My
first mental collapse

came on me like fog during a
student party. I walked through the
rain until the following afternoon.

Innominate Tarn: a dawn-
release of an isolated population
Micropsectra midges, precipitated
by acid fallout from Sellafield.
Innominate Tarn: no name

as a name, a glittering alphabet
of haiku in water's Japanese form:
'The tarn spoke her name / without
name, a midge's mute / syllable of
blood.'

A PhD in the pH scale of
Lakeland tarns, from acid to
limestone, from summit to corrie.
As I counted the million

million diatoms under my
microscope I grew unable to think
of living things as having existence
other than in a fury of data.

Innominate Tarn: imagine a
surface area of zones, niches of
seasonal insect variations, midge-
vortices, submarine

rocks, and stones, and trees, flooded
cairns, cloud-crowns, and mayfly-
days as long as twenty days are
now.

THE APOSTLE BIRDS
In memory of Les Murray

*In Shakespeare's birth chamber in Stratford on Avon a glass panel
exposes wattle-and-daub between beams*

there are twelve   no
        there are thirteen
                apostle birds

scribbling with their beaks
        the gooey manures
                nabbed from a dewpond edge

snaffling straws of sedge
        from the parched australian bush
                dabbing sun-dappled mush

testing and tasting and pasting
        the glues of a nest-cup
                with their plastering

perimetering beak-trowels
        the whole gang
                goes up – BLAM! – as One

and lands again
      as Three – bickering
            jokily jostling

over a job
      their selfless genes
            squawked sod's law at

the apostle birds
      go on scrappily
            scrabbling and shaping

their small world's whorl
      of muck-and-straw
            of happy dung and all

in which their featherless
      brawling shakespeares
            will gape and call

I DROPT DOWN ON THE THYMY MOLEHILL

'I wandered the heath in raptures among the rabbit burrows
& golden blossomd furze
I dropt down on the thymy molehill' – John Clare

'Conies', whispers Wisdom Smith, 'require calm,
dawn-craft and a down-wind'. 'While my riming,'
murmurs John Clare, 'obliges a simpler psalm.
I cannot sing for breakfast when ravening.'

Both men flex their full shanks before kneeling.
They paw the grass aside and slide askew
like stoats slinking sidelong toward their prey
before the hell's mouths of the warren's holes.

Rabbits rebound from a moor russet with molehills.
Bucks nip, dash, stamp, scrabble, scuffle.
Kittens suckle under dozing, sun-stunned does.

'As if Heaven fell and Hell erupted on the same acre'
whistles the Gypsy, fitting the musket to his shoulder
while chewing softly on the stalk of a cuckooflower.

ξ

My vow babbles with quicksilver bubbles of an Otter.
  My vow caws in a beech tree's apoplectic rookery.

Your vow catches the pin-drop of a Pine Marten pattering over pine-needles.
  Your vow dodges with a Dipper weaving whirlpools under-river.

Your vow scribes a root-word, the speech tablet of a beech tree.
  Your vow prises a Crossbill's Fibonacci tines of a pinecone.

My vow is Emily Dickinson's meadow-harvested herbarium.
  My vow torrents through rain-cleaved clints and grykes.

My vow is a child's wordlessness. My vow can be their fury.
  My vow is Emily Dickinson's love-note: 'everyone else is prose.'

Your vow shapes keepsakes from a baby's nearly and early words.
  Your vow moves the Mohs Scale from mica to lapis lazuli.

Your vow is a Pangolin pengguling into dragon-scales,
  and slumbers with an Arctic Wolf's snowball-pawed, trigger-clawed cubs.

THE CARAVANS OF TARSHISH

Silver spread into plates is brought from Tarshish,
and gold from Uphaz, the work of the workman,
and of the hands of the founder: blue and purple
is their clothing: they are all the work of cunning men.
– Jeremiah 10: 9

'The funeral of "The Prince of Gypsies, Wisdom Smith," aged 76, took place at Essendine, in Rutland, on the 4th inst. About one hundred of the wandering tribe were present at the ceremony, and a large concourse of peasantry from the adjacent villages also joined the burial train. The dark faced outcasts, in projecting this spectacle, were wiser in their generation than the simple rustics among whom they had pitched their tents; they secured a "comfortable coffin" for their patriarch by assuring the joiner that the "Prince's son was worth thousands" and that he would come from the north to take the place of chief mourner in the obsequies. They also duped other small tradesmen by assuring them that the wealthy heir to the vacant diadem of their … people would pay for everything in a most princely manner! Every man, woman, and child of the crafty race, however, had disappeared like a mist before the morning succeeding the ceremony, and the tradesmen are unpaid.'

Lincolnshire Mercury, Saturday 27 April 1839

Christian names and tribal surnames of the Roma in the caravans were current at the time the story is set; as are the English titles for professions and occupations.

1ˢᵗ caravan

Laverock All Alone of all the Crafters
Northward and Sherebiah of the Nails

Wainwright and Saffron of the Wheelers
Queenie Rose and Darkle of the Carterleays

Evergreen and Loolodì of the Burrs
Innocence and Diaphaney of the Stanleys

Studivares and Paradise of the Applebys
Archippus and Angelis of the Lavenders

Trafalgar and Fidelity of the Raffertys
and of the true Lees   no word

His word,

his hòrata gallops to his son at Kirkby Stephen:
the Prince has fallen into the phoov of mourning.

The Prince's son is to bolt from his camps,
headlong to his place as chief mourner in the obsequies.

Hòrata returns at a clip on a Lipizzaner
splattering down dales, the Great North Road –

his Lanórdo Drom.

hòrata: the word, the message; **phoov**: land; **Lanórdo**: North; **drom**: road

2nd caravan

Thuhash and Bibiyaka of the Badgers
Levi and Mary Defiance of the Burtons

Greenleaf and Galatia of the Faas
Salathiel and Starlini of the Viney Boswells

Damon and Angrydolly of Les Bas
Perpagelion Widower of the Poles

Purify of the Barrington Bucklands
Tyson and The Magician of the Furies

Sinfi and No-Sin of the Herons
and of the Throstles   only Mad Throstle

Hurtling, tarrying

from Appleby Kirk to Kirk Yetholm to Stow-on-the Wold
all tarry on his hòrata, both tribe-child and tribe-foal.

Toward him are mine eyes; or to him are my fountains.
He is the cheshmyà, yokker of an indais, our habitation.

The Prince of the Rom is dead. Long live the cshavò of his sect.
Long-proven are his people, long-primed the son's pockets,

saddlebags splitting with silver chinìya and pearls.
Sovnà alchemises before him: stepping stones across rivers;

Roman droms hammered into Sarn Helen and Stanage.

A permanent putèka.

cheshmyà: fountain; yokker: the eye; indais: the people; cshavò: son;
chinìya: plate; sovnà: gold; putèka: pathway

3rd caravan

Samson and Old Sorrow of the Scamps
Robin and Rubicon of the Robinsons

Simeon and Shadrach of the Scarrotts
Philologus and Olympas of the Perfects

Pyramus and Prudence of the Proudleys
Alladin and Shiva of the Orchards

Zadok and Patience of the Norths
Sallow and Sloe of the Whimpennies

Zebra and Plenti of the Packwoods
and of the Key Harvester   no word

Hastyàv of a rumour, a mummed message between Roma.
Yet we make sure Rumour takes a dive into the doonyàs.

Rumour's spawnier than trout rivers:
our cshib slops and rolls right over bryàgoos.

Rumour speeds to the River Ouse, ferries it
to Kings Lynn and by parila makes sail

to our tribes in the Kent hop-fields, our indais of the kale.

hastyàv: a yawn; **doonyàs**: world; **cshib**: speech; **bryàgoos**: river-banks;
parila: nightfall

Rumour flows across floodplains of the shires,
surges across Warwickshire and Worcestershire

to leap in Herefordshire – macshò to makhì –
wind down the Wye, sweep we down the Severn.

Zàprezi at vardos holed-up in holloways of Cymru.

macshò: fish; makhì: fly; zàprezi: stop (imperative); vardo: Gypsy
caravan

4th caravan

Thurles Strawson of the Thatchers
Starling and Speedwell of the Ferns

Achilles and Charity of the Slaughters
Slim Sarah Duty of the Swans

Wacka and Woodlock of the Mallets
Kedar and Darklis of the Kemps

Ochennia Alone of the Downlands
Bartholoways and Britannia of the Stonewalls

Uriel and Sidh of the Rivers
and of the Englands   no word

Clishmaclavar!

Gypsy fever fires up Stamford market. Traders
trip from stall to stall, nudging neighbours.

Shop-boys pelt down country lanes for advance orders.
All supplies are on slate; all slates swept spotless.

The shopkeepers wipe their counters, wax the tips
of their moustaches. Preen into mirrors – into profits.

Stamford glows as ovens seethe and grumble.
Sugar-cones are shaved. Pans babble with jams.

Grease slops from roasting spits. Pinnies are spattered;
pigs bludgeoned, bled, scalded, butchered.

Pies pressed out; blood puddings pounded,
stuffed into gut with a snap of two thumbs.

Stamford snuffles like a swine gone scavenging.
Huge hams are heaved from smoking hooks

slid slumped, slammed down,
severed on clot-smeared carving blocks.

5ᵗʰ caravan

Jonah and Sanspirela of the Floodgates
Siskin and Honesty of the Elys

Isaac and Tryphosa of the Tilers
Gabriel and Virtue of the Laughters

Edward and Cinderella of the Dearloves
Harefoot and Zhanna of the Keenans

Pharaoh and Poratha of the Heaths
Adamant and Eros of the Jobs

Righteous Rose Nipkin of the Christmases
and of the Shepsters   no word

Rom of the nor'western vrehòolka approaches,
cheshmyà of him that they called or prayed,

with sovnà from Uphaz, the graft of their craftsmen.

And in the doss-alleys by the city koorkò –

Rom: the Gypsy; **vrehòolka**: storm; **koorkò**: market

Pudding-men scuttle

lofting their laden trays above steaming manure heaps.
Loaves bustle in brimming baskets. Not one baker sleeps.

From Lound and Langtoft, Maxey and Northborough
tramp Costermongers, Dripping Men, Knockknobblers.

From Aunby and Helpston, Braceborough and Glinton
gad Farandmen, Fishdryvers, Prig Nappers.

From Barholm, Carlby and Tickencote,
slope Schrimpschongers, Snobscats, Stravaigers.

Costermonger: fruit seller; Dripping Man: dealer in dripping (the fat collected during the cooking of meats); Knockknobbler: dog catcher; Farandman: travelling merchant; Fishdryver: victualler; Prig Napper: horse thief; Schrimpschonger: artisan who carves in bone, ivory, or wood; Snobscat: shoe-repairer; Stravaiger: vagrant

Shoemakers at their ale-slops with Warren-keepers,
Sheargrinders, Skeppers, Saw Doctors,

upwind of Tanners yakking flapdoodle with Fripperers.
Clarissa of Cock's Lane on the granite arm of a Plowman,

sole soul who could tally the tithes of any man.

Puffing her clay pipe as she tut-tuts at the Kerfuffle.

Sheargrinder: sharpener of shears, scythes and scissors; **Skepper**: maker
and seller of beehives; **Saw Doctor**: maker and maintainer a wide range
of cutting tools and saw blades; **Fripperers**: buyer and seller of old
clothes

6th caravan

Damage and Atonement of the Mountains
Deedrik and Antichrist of the Sansoms

Temperance and Salvation of the Hearnes
Belshazzar and Liberty of the Skeets

Egypt and Vashti of the Wesseldines
Archangel and Arden of the Atchings

Damaris and Siberetta of the Fletchers
Malachi and Pomona of the Meadows

Daedca and Esmeralda of the Roadmakers
and of the Black Smiths   no word

Wisdom Smith, departed prince, pral to poet John Clare;
moosì across his chill chest in Saint Mary Magdalene –

stirs in death-life, lifts kiepachì, time-travelling. *Aye.*
Domesday sees Barthi hold Essendine with sake and soke,

land for 6 ploughs, one slave, one mill
and 3 acres of meadows; a woodland. Wisdom

smiles to himself as his vogi wakes in 1839. Elsewhere
Daguerre holds up the first photograph of the moon,

Thomas Henderson steers his eye through Alpha Centauri
and John Clare weeps under Northampton Asylum's vaulted sky.

pral: best pal; **moosì**: arms; **kiepachì**: eyelids; **vogi**: soul

Dead-drunk Gentiles lìndra in the ginnels of Essendine.
A weshjook snuffs and flinches from campfires of Gypsies.

The char under Wisdom's vardo is still smouldering.
Mahrimé, his bed was broken, the bracken slighted.

Father of princes, he alights in the phoov called morning.
King on a chessboard moving any old way, one move at a...

the Rom's soul scuds through space and time.
Ever the way with Wisdom, *aye*, ever the way –

Wisdom Smith Prince of Gypsies
b. Steeple Claydon 1763

d. Essendine 1839.

As if.

lìndra: snooze; weshjook: dog-fox; char: grass; mahrimé: defiled,
unclean

7th caravan

Angel and Alice of the Woodlanders
Evening and Salome of the Slenders

Soul and Cleopatra of the Waterfields
Loudly and Sage of the True Boswells

Temperance and Tabitha of the Newburys
Salvino and Mercy of the Hamms

Old Oswestry and Offa of the Welsh
Simpronius Bohemia of the Borders

Nemo Alone of the Loveless
and of the Winters   no word.

This world is thrush-song, linnet-bustle in mayflower.
Geese grizzle on the pond with hung-over necks.

Tilth gleams in Essendine churchyard.
A robin frisks fresh grave-soil – her larder.

A storm-cock stands weathervane to St Mary's tower
circling with the breeze to cast skied notes further.

Siskins pick at gravestones. Church bells strike four.

A song-thrush starts over over over.
Vardos with wheel-rims lulled in sackcloth

harnessed to ponies, hooves hushed with saddlecloth,
sigh like a river over smoothed cobbles of the lanes

breaching the boundary where roads radiate,
spokes spinning to the rims of wide England;

sober Roma stare back at dozing Essendine.
No Gentile rouses from drowsing houses.

No body drawn from earth-dark at dawn.

A man leaps from the face of the sun.

A man leaps from the face of the sun.

Silver spread into plates is brought from Tarshish
and gold from Uphaz, the graft of the workman,

and of the hands of the founder: blue and purple
is their clothing: they are all the work of cunning men.

I lifted up mine eyes, I looked, and beheld:

a wise man clothed in linen, girded with fine gold.

Nemo Alone

Simpronius Bohemia

Old Oswestry and Offa

Salvino and Mercy

Temperance and Tabitha

Loudly and Sage

Soul and Cleopatra

Evening and Salome

Angel and Alice

Daedca and Esmeralda

Malachi and Pomona

Damaris and Siberetta

Archangel and Arden

Egypt and Vashti

Belshazzar and Liberty

Temperance and Salvation

Deedrik and Antichrist

Damage and Atonement

Righteous Rose Nipkin

Adamant and Eros

Pharaoh and Poratha

Harefoot and Zhanna

Edward and Cinderella

Gabriel and Virtue

Isaac and Tryphosa

Siskin and Honesty

Jonah and Sanspirela

                        Uriel and Sidh
        Bartholoways and Britannia
                        Ochennia Alone
                    Kedar and Darklis
    Wacka and Woodlock
                        Slim Sarah Duty
            Achilles and Charity
                    Starling and Speedwell
        Thurles Strawson
                    Zebra and Plenti
    Sallow and Sloe
                        Zadok and Patience
                Alladin and Shiva
                    Pyramus and Prudence
        Philologus and Olympas
                        Simeon and Shadrach
    Robin and Rubicon
                    Samson and Old Sorrow
            Sinfi and No-Sin
                        Tyson and The Magician
        Purify is Purity alone
                        Perpagelion Widower
            Damon and Angrydolly
                        Salathiel and Starlini
    Greenleaf and Galatia
                Levi and Mary Defiance
                        Thuhash and Bibiyaka
        Trafalgar and Fidelity
                    Archippus and Angelis
            Studivares and Paradise

Innocent and Diaphaney
Evergreen and Loolodì
Queenie Rose and Darkle
Wainwright and Saffron
Northward and Sherebiah
Laverock All Alone

and of The Prince of Gypsies?

no word

KOP KOP TO HIS HORSES HE SINGS AND NO MORE
(John Clare)

Five hours of slither, flank-shiver and slip.
Wisdom Smith flips the foal, tensions a birth-rope,
hauls hind-limbs hard-about, solar surfaces
of the hooves face up. Now. Wisdom delivers
snout-first, forelimbs shying air, all four
swinging, swaying down on to bloody straw.
'There's my Light of Lights!' laughs the Gypsy.
'Lightest of hoof, lit-through with all her mother!'

'You love them like your own', whispers John Clare.
John kneels by the foal and by his man of air.
'That's them free', gasps Wisdom. 'All family.
Nothing cleaves you from the face you first see'.
The mare sniffs and slathers her child's eyes.
Her foal staggers, and blinks as if surprised.

CHERRY PICKERS

Dale Farm Traveller Site Eviction

A kestrel spears sidelong on a thermal above the camp
clasping and unclenching the load-bearings of his claws.

Eyes harrow the grass with ultraviolet vision:
runnels or trapdoors for voles and field-mice

iridescent in the hovering kestrel's retina.
Down the bird plummets. Sunlight strews her wands.

The JCB tears down the caravan's door,
slams down its prongs, shakes its claw.

'What's the load-bearing for a Pikey's caravan?
These fruit pickers' vardos, they're built like bastard houses.'

Prying for weakness the bailiff stabs a corner,
twists prongs, tilts on caterpillar treads, grips,

and rips the roof from a Traveller family
breakfasting together as sunlight strews

wands through the field and hedgerows
beyond their caravan's still-opened windows.

Out spill internal organs of a botched operation:
the proudly folded teak dining table,

a chandelier's glittering sprawl and glory,
a cupboard loud with Royal Doulton,

the pot belly stove still toasty from the morning.
The cherry pickers lift their arms into the sun.

Cherry pickers: mobile elevating work platforms for removing protestors

OUR HOME IS A HUNGER

Ma, Pa, the two girls and Nan, share their breakfast
of Joey Gray. The girls tug lumps from the plump loaf,

swabbing and shining their soup bowls. Nan says,
'Half my hunger is gone. Half my life is grown.

And one still grows and the other goes.
It is time.' Nan holds her granddaughters' hands.

'Life is a rare road, mother', the Gypsy father replies
shrugging at the dawn, 'We have tarried too long.

Our home is a hunger too. This world is gone.'
Sunlight strews her wands and watches on.

All the nameless people named here.
The story ends with who we were.

ξ

SEVENTH LYREBIRD

My vow glints with deer-hooves daring beyond a treeline.
My vow ambles like an Anteater between turrets of termites.

My vow slinks with the dog-fox behind the prints and prince of rabbits.
My vow blinks from field's flints among frozen tares.

Your vow trips a honey-badger with motion-capture cameras.
Your vow trepans tectonics from a mountain's memory.

Your vow is Raymond Carver posting the word hummingbird in a letter.
Your vow traces bloody paw-tracks to – where? – this grizzling bear.

My vow grasps a glacier's crevasse and verglas.
My vow climbs Amazonian trees on a Hoatzin's dinosaur-winged fingers.

My vow is Tess Gallagher holding the hummingbird of summer.
Our vow sings the names we share with our children.

Your vow clutches the Hoatzin's hapless fledglings in an Amazonian river.
My vow is the Lyrebird's thesaurus of memory.

TRANSLATIONS FROM A STAMMERER

after a phrase by Anna Akhmatova

I like owl-lamps to be left burning in each room,
bedroom doors ajar after owl-dark,
the hearth-fire hooting like an owl up the chimney.

You lift and light the lantern of an owl,
open the owl-door, switch on the owl-light.
The garden flickers with filaments of owl-flight.

Tear down our moon, Owl, with your talons and talons.

after a phrase by Osip Mandelshtam

    I inhaled
your white breath in the fog of the river's mouth

when you talked to me of the river's mouth
you walked as a child

we are too far inland
I can't follow you along a shore of a river's mouth

your estuaries are in exile
wave after wave of landmass drowns you in the river's mouth

you weep when you hear the waves of the ocean lapping the river's mouth

after a phrase by Paul Celan

~~an innocent lyre, my therapist wrote~~
~~'a stammer is wound through the heart'~~
an innocent liar, my therapist wrote
'a stammer is a wound to the heart'

~~i can only stammer these words~~
~~my tongue has become a liar's bird~~
i can only stammer these words
my tongue has become a lyre's bird

after a phrase by Bronisława Wajs

how your heart half-hears
        my stammer
within the hemisphere
        of your heart's ear

after a phase by Marina Tsvetaeva

        i climb to the crown of an apple tree
                in the old cider orchard
        the one ancient tree remaining
                of three hundred
        grasp apple-heavy branches in my fists
                shuddering fruit
        into the leaf shaded shirts and shawls
                of my glad friends

        th–th–there is enough in heaven

79

after a phrase by Vladimir Mayakovsky

anechoic larynx
    of a stammerer
        where speech
slept in a chamber
    below a whiplashed tongue
        yet words flowered
in parch
    harking for
        the rain-lashed

    rose of the mouth

after a phrase by Bronisława Wajs

spoken word?

written words offer no rest
speech is not woken by breath

slam this book shut

wordlessness

after a phrase by John Keats

after Anna Akhmatova and Paul Celan
after Bronisława Wajs and Mayakovsky
after Mandelshtam and Marina Tsvetaeva

after i hid my living hand
under their living hands
(see, here they are)

     i held it out to you

Romani words are pronounced exactly as they appear.

The use of the term 'Romany' and 'Romani' are used interchangeably depending on context.

THE THROWN VOICE. *Uncle* is a term of respect by younger travellers towards older Roma men, used here by the teenage Traveller mockingly.

ROMANY WOUNDS ME. A Romani English interpretation of George Seferis's 'In the Manner of G. S.': 'Wherever I travel Greece wounds me'; 'Meanwhile, Greece keeps on travelling, always travelling...', translated by Edmund Keeley and Philip Sherrard.

FURY. Adapted from interviews with Tyson Fury, the British Gypsy professional boxer, one of the main sources being an interview with Donald McRae in *Guardian*, 5 November 2011. Tyson openly spoke about the racial abuse he receives by being a Gypsy World Champion, because 'nobody wants to see a Gypsy do well'. Tyson also said, 'I'd like to take a course in writing. I'm not the best writer in the world.' 'The best style is no style' – Bruce Lee.

THE KEY HARVEST. 'I am what her savage loving has made me, and it is good that one of us should accept that finally' – letter by Samuel Beckett, writing of his mother: *Damned to Fame: The Life of Samuel Beckett* by James Knowlson.

AFTER THE BURIAL OF THE MATRIARCH. The language used is a contemporary English dialect of Romani. After death, the van and belongings of a Roma Gypsy are considered *marime*, that is 'unclean', and are burnt. Many Roma families are led by older women, a role passed from mother to daughter to granddaughter, their wisdom based on experience and memory rather than written word. 'What the Roma do not say to each other is buried in mirnomos' centres on a Roma belief that writing anything down can be seen as dangerous, or disloyal. After the Roma Holocaust – also known as the *Porajmos* which means 'The Devouring' – when over 1 million Roma were murdered, few accounts of the event were written by Roma. Their silence – their shared *mirnomos* – was because the *Porajmos* was regarded as *marime*.

THE STUTTERING BUTCHER AND THE SUGARBEET KING. This ballad is adapted from the words of "Wisdom ('Wiggy') Smith (1926–2001)" by Gwilym Davies, *Folk Music Journal*, Annual 2004: 'Wiggy was one of the last of the English Traveller singers to sing old songs in the old style. Wiggy was born in a covered wagon near Bristol in the days when roadside gypsies were a more common sight than nowadays. His family travelled around the West Midlands area in a horse-drawn trailer and knew true poverty of a kind which is rare today. He and his family ended up in Gloucestershire where he lived until his death, although he always claimed that his family roots were in Hampshire. The many skills he learnt in his lifetime included how to converse in Romany, how to fit a wheel on a wagon, how to go ferreting for rabbits and how to find the best edible mushrooms. At one time, he earned a living as a prize-fighter and remained fit and strong into his seventies. He spent his life living on his wits to provide for his wife Myra and large family. As Wiggy himself said, 'The money wasn't about, but it was better times all round.' His descendants amounted to over a hundred at his death, including great-grandchildren, all of whom he adored with fierce pride.'

STARLING ROOST IN SWANSEA. 'Igam Ogam'. Welsh slang: to zig-zag drunkenly. Derived from *Igam Ogam*, a Welsh pre-school stop motion animated television series.

WHEN I HEARD THE CALLING OF BIRDS. Towfiq Bihani has been held in Guantánamo Bay Detention Centre since early 2003 despite having never been charged with a crime. In 2010, Towfiq was officially cleared for release by the Obama administration yet he still remains detained. Towfiq writes poetry in English and Arabic. One of Towfiq's poems closes with the line, 'When I heard the calling of birds, I remembered your sweet voice when you sang the song "remember me this way"'. I took the line as my starting point for a poem in the form of a ghazal. All the birds invoked in the poem live in Guantánamo Naval Base which, paradoxically, is a haven for wildlife.

SIGNIFICANCE AT INNOMINATE TARN. In my twenties I carried out research on the impact of acid rain on Chironomid communities in tarns of the English Lake Ditsrict. *Chironomidae* are non-biting midges adapted to live in a vast range of aquatic habitats. 'A beauty neither of fine colour nor long eyelash, nor pencilled brow, but of meaning, of movement, of radiance.' – Charlotte Brontë, *Jane Eyre*. 'Sweet childish days, that were as long / as twenty days are now!' – William Wordsworth, 'To a Butterfly'.

THE APOSTLE BIRDS. Australian Apostle Birds will gang up with six to twenty other birds, doing everything together, team-building a single nest, and telling each other about it very loudly.

LYREBIRDS. For Siobhan Keenan.

'The lyrebird sings one of the longest, most melodious and complex of all bird songs. The males have become superlative mimics…a skilled ornithologist may be able to recognise the songs of over a dozen other birds embedded in the lyrebird's incomparable recitals. Some individuals have territories close to those occupied by human beings and they incorporate the new sounds they hear coming across their frontiers. So they include in their performances accurate imitations of such things as spot-welding machines, burglar alarms and camera motor drives.' – Sir David Attenborough

'How could I possibly join them on to the little bit (two Inches wide) of Ivory on which I work with so fine a Brush, as produces little effect after much labour? – Jane Austen. The 'little bit of ivory' was a slim pocket notebook composed of pieces of ivory bound together and on which she could make notes in pencil and later erase.

'I spilt the dew –
But took the morn –
I chose this single star
From out the wide night's numbers –
Sue – forevermore!'
'One Sister have I in our house' – Emily Dickinson

'This is why I value that little phrase "I don't know" so highly. It's small, but it flies on mighty wings. It expands our lives to include the spaces within us as well as those outer expanses in which our tiny Earth hangs suspended.' – 'The Poet and the World', Nobel Prize lecture, 1996, Wisława Szymborska

'I often wondered what my grandmother knew that none of the rest of us knew and if she alone knew it, or if it was a

total mystery that really nobody knew except perhaps God.'
– Elizabeth Bishop

'On me your voice falls as they say love should,
Like an enormous yes.'
– 'For Sidney Bichet', Philip Larkin

                                'It's evident
the art of losing's not too hard to master
though it may look like (*Write* it!) like disaster.'
– 'One Art', Elizabeth Bishop

'To see a World in a Grain of Sand
And a Heaven in a Wild Flower
Hold Infinity in the palm of your hand
And Eternity in an hour'
'Auguries of Innocence' – William Blake

'The flight is safe; the weather is all arranged.
The waves are running in verses this fine morning.
Please come flying.'
'Invitation to Miss Marianne Moore' – Elizabeth Bishop

'All of you in a space full of sounds – in the shade and in the
light. You were called AUXOCHROME the one who captures
colour. I CHROMOPHORE – the one who gives colour.'
– Frida Kahlo, from a letter to Diego de Rivera

'My only desire's a desire
to be

free from desire.'
'Desire's a Desire' – Selima Hill

'A belt of straw and Ivy buds,
With Coral clasps and Amber studs:
And if these pleasures may thee move,
Come live with me, and be my love.'
'The Passionate Shepherd to His Love'
– Christopher Marlowe

'You perhaps at one time thought there was such a thing as worldly happiness to be arrived at, at certain periods of time marked out – you have of necessity from your disposition been thus led away – I scarcely remember counting upon any Happiness – I look not for it if it be not in the present hour – nothing startles me beyond the moment. The Setting Sun will always set me to rights, or if a Sparrow come before my Window, I take part in its existence and pick about the gravel.' – John Keats, from a letter to Benjamin Bailey, 22 November 1817

'I almost wish we were butterflies and liv'd but three summer days – three such days with you I could fill with more delight than fifty common years could ever contain.' – John Keats, from a letter to Fanny Brawne, Newport, July 3, 1819

'We are the only poets, and everyone else is *prose*.'
– Emily Dickinson, from a letter to Susan Gilbert

The Mohs scale of mineral hardness is a qualitative ordinal scale characterizing scratch resistance of various minerals through the ability of harder material to scratch softer material.

'All the world will be your enemy, Prince with a Thousand Enemies, and whenever they catch you, they will kill you. But first they must catch you, digger, listener, runner, prince

with the swift warning. Be cunning and full of tricks and your
people shall never be destroyed'
– Richard Adams, *Watership Down*

'Only one mountain can know the core of another mountain'
– Frida Kahlo, from a letter to Diego de Rivera

'Suppose I say summer,
write the word "hummingbird,"
put it in an envelope,
take it down the hill
to the box. When you open
my letter you will recall
those days and how much,
just how much, I love you.'
'Hummingbird' – Raymond Carver

Hoatzin (South America): Their chicks have claws on two
of their wing digits, an adaptation shared by *Archaeopteryx*.
Parent Hoatzins build their nest over streams: when in danger
nestlings jump into the stream, swim underwater, and climb
another tree to safety.

CHERRY PICKERS and OUR HOME IS A HUNGER.
At 7a.m. on 19 October 2011 the site clearance of Dale Farm
Traveller Camp began. Electricity was disconnected. More
than one hundred riot police entered the site through the rear
fence and two people were tasered. Police removed Travellers
from the twelve-metre high scaffold tower on the front
gate with 'cherry pickers', mobile elevating work platforms.
Travellers are often employed as fruit pickers and packers.

ACKNOWLEDGEMENTS

Thanks are due to the editors of the following publications in which some of these poems, or versions of them, have previously appeared: *Modern Poetry in Translation, Poetry Salzburg, Poetry Wales, Travellers' Times, The Death of Wisdom Smith Prince of Gypsies* (The Melos Press).

'When I Heard the Calling of Birds' was commissioned by Reprieve and the Ledbury Poetry Festival. 'Honour' was commissioned for *Metamorphic: 21st century poets respond to Ovid* edited by Nessa O'Mahony and Paul Munden. 'What Will You Give for the Moon?' appeared on Carol Ann Duffy's WRITE where we are NOW website responding to the Covid-19 pandemic.

Grateful thanks to Siobhan Keenan, William Palmer, Pascale Petit, Michael Schmidt.